Is that a counselor in your pocket or are you just happy?

Gary Pignatello, LCSW

For Jessica, Jazzy , & Aiden
You bring meaning to it all

Forward

Sometime around 1983, I found myself back living with my parents. They lived a thousand miles away from where I had lived and where I was comfortable. Needless to say, great success wasn't the reason for my situation. I was hoping to spend some time under their roof as a respite from the mess I'd created elsewhere and as an opportunity to take stock and plan my next move. It was a good plan. Easy. Doable. Sensible. But none of those things guided me a day up to that point, and they wouldn't in the 34 years since.

One evening during that time, I was watching an episode of the sitcom The Jeffersons. That particular episode was about George Jefferson becoming a millionaire. While watching the show a small, faint voice in my head said, "Wow, I bet a lot of people in the real world have had similar success in their lives". After that percolated a bit, a loud, booming voice (still in my head) shouted out, "MANY PEOPLE HAVE GONE FROM RAGS TO RICHES, WHY CAN'T YOU??" Ridiculous as it was, that was a turning point in my life. I left my parents house, moved a thousand miles back to the place I'd made my life previously, and started the slow and steady journey that I've been on ever since.

That silly story is relevant because it's the best example, in my life anyway, of how to use this book. The episode of the Jeffersons wasn't particularly deep or uplifting. It was a great show but it wasn't meant to be anything but funny. And that episode was not unusual in any way compared to the hundreds of episodes that preceded it. So why then did it have such a significant impact on me? The answer is, timing. It was admittedly a typically anemic sitcom episode, but it reached me at exactly the right time. So, the formula is:

Weak Message + Great Timing = Sea Change

The secret to success, right? Unfortunately, no. The formula works, I have no doubt about that and you've probably had similar experiences. But there's a problem. We can't create or anticipate when the right time will be. There is, however, another side to that coin. We can't anticipate when the right time will come, but we *can* keep positive messages around us so when it does come it will have something to grab onto and slingshot us in the right direction. This book is a tool for doing just that.

I call this a "Flip-To Book" (I think I coined that term). The way a flip-to book works is, when you are feeling down/confused/unsure, flip it open to a random page and read the message. Perhaps it'll have no meaning for you at all, but maybe it'll be the right message at the right time. Perhaps it'll be your George Jefferson! If nothing else, it's good to keep positive messages around us and this book is an opportunity to create the habit.

I hope something in here leads to a positive shift in your life. Something significant that provides a silly and wonderful story of your own. If not I hope you at least have fun reading it.

Best of Life

Gary Pignatello

The person making the most noise is usually doing the least work

Let go of your thoughts for 2 minutes. Let go of things you have to do, let go of your troubles

Just be still

Am I ovrly critical?

Planning is always valuable

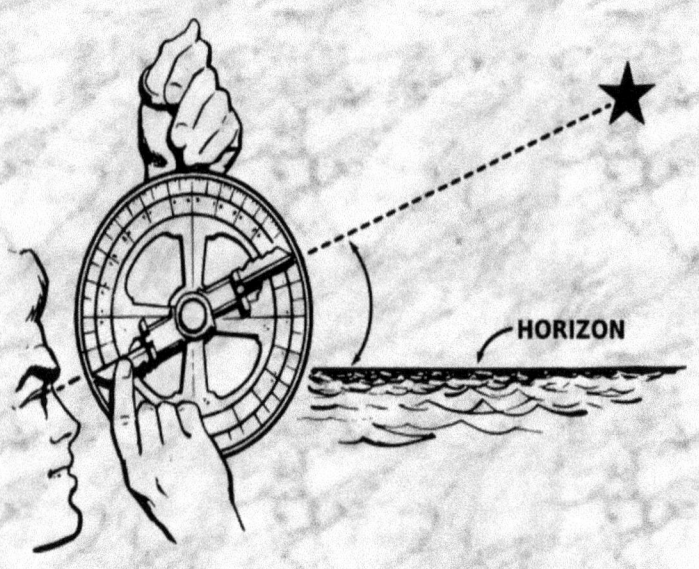

whether you follow through or not

When is enough, enough?

Now?

Will you even remember this in ten years?

Is it better to be happy

or right?

You were born worthy

Period!

Do you truly need it?

If you have choices

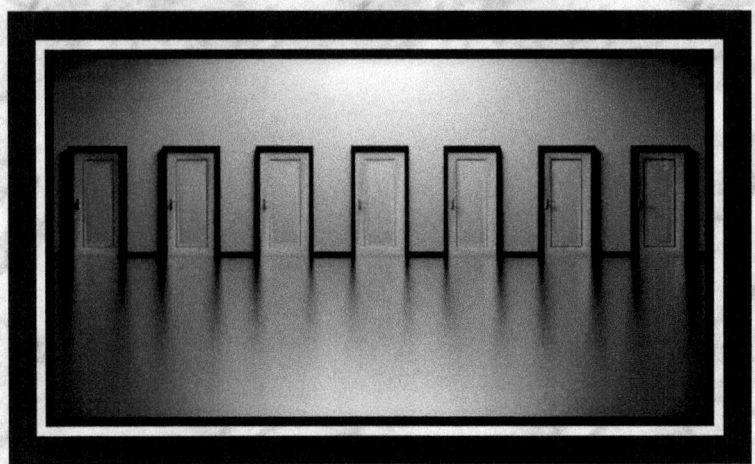

you have freedom

**If you
have to decide right
now
say**

Everyone is afraid

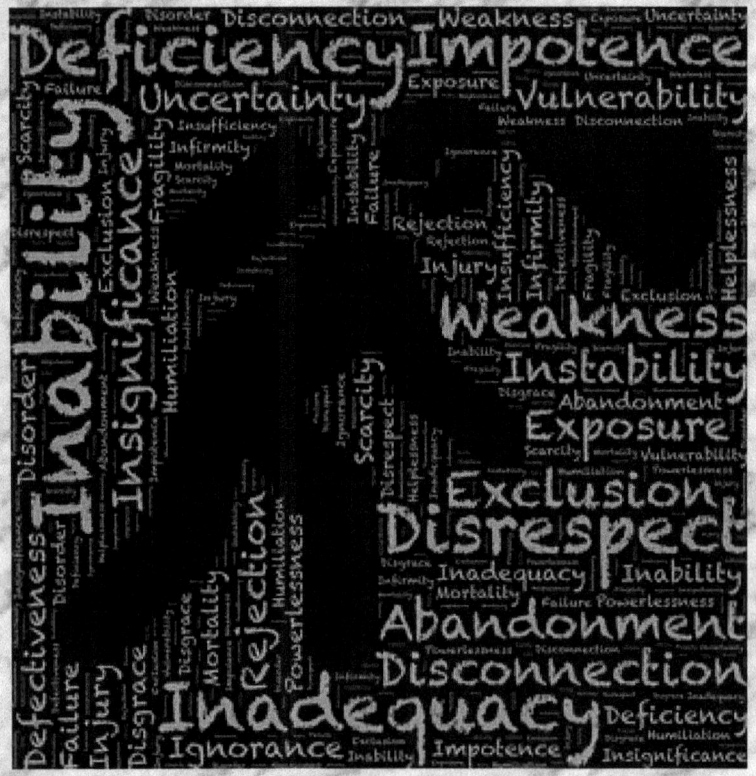

Do it anyway

Your attitude will follow your face

Life isn't a competition

so don't make it one

Choose an object that's near you and focus on it for a minute or two. It can be anything. Don't do anything except notice what you are looking at and relax

Clench your fist and slowly breathe into your fingers.

Ask yourself, "what's possible today?"

Spend ten or fifteen minutes in complete silence.

Use earplugs

You are what you pretend to be

Name 2 things that make you feel good

1. _____

2. _____

Silently repeat a short prayer, religious phrase, or a non-religious affirmation

Stop what you're doing and go for a walk

Relax,

let it unfold

in its own time

Let her Go

This too shall pass

All you need has been in you since the day you were born

You're already great. Now go out and show them just how great

Lead, Follow,

Or Get out of the way

WAKE UP!

You're made of stardust

Act like it

Your direction is infinitely more important than your speed

Police your thoughts, they quickly turn into things

It's all in your approach

Question

The wall is high

But
my
arms
are
strong

If there is no struggle

there is no progress

The hunter will remain the hero until the lion learns to write

A thick skin is more valuable than a quick tongue

**Hang in
Winter always ends
and spring always
follows**

Never underestimate the power of a day dream

It ain't personal, its just life

Make your own luck

Sometimes you must stand

alone

Perspective

Don't make permanent decisions about temporary problems

What are you getting out of this?

Go, Just Go

Whose rules are they anyway?

They can only win if you give-in to hate

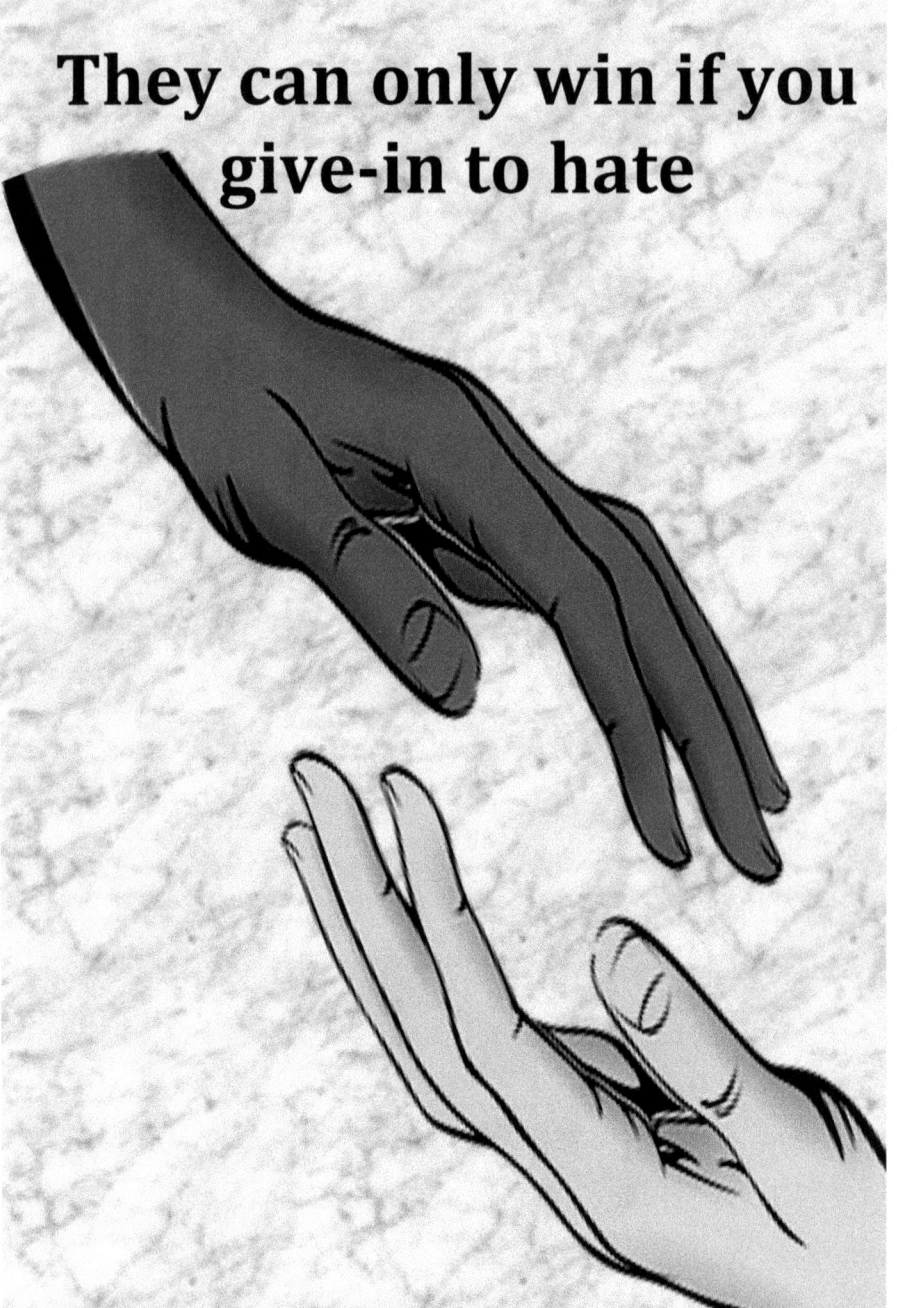

Every hero has a story

what will yours be?

Create your own narrative

Gratitude is always possible

If you can't decide which to choose, choose love

Hold the door for someoneand notice their reaction

Try going out to eat alone

Say hi to 3 strangers each day

Write a negative event or emotion on a piece of paper. Go outside, put that paper in a lighted grill and watch it burn to ashes.

No matter what, be kind to yourself

Be
The
Adult

Write letters you never intend to send

Losing is as reliable as the sunrise Embrace it

Disloyalty belittles them, not you

If counting to 10 doesn't work, count to 100

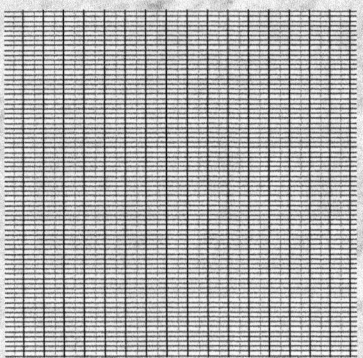

1000
10,000

Never peck the dirt with chickens when you can ride the winds with eagles

When things seem out of control

do something ordinary like shave or food shop

Go to a movie by yourself

Write 3 or 4 things you strive for on an index card. Put it in a private place and read it from time to time

Fear is a mountain that must be climbed

Your thoughts are like a sail on a windy day. They will carry you far

Slow to judge

Slow to condemn

Quick to forgive

What are you looking at?

At any meal you have today, when you take the first bite take a minute and pay attention to the taste, the texture, the temperature.

Yawn and stretch for 10 seconds. Try to do this several times each day.

Wrap your arms around yourself and give yourself a tight hug. Maintain the hug through 3 breaths.

Sit in a chair with feet flat on the floor and notice how your feet feel inside your socks, notice how they feel in your shoes, how they feel against the ground. Turn your attention to your lower legs and move up to your upper legs noticing how they feel.

One day I will die
But on every other day
I will live

If not now, then when?

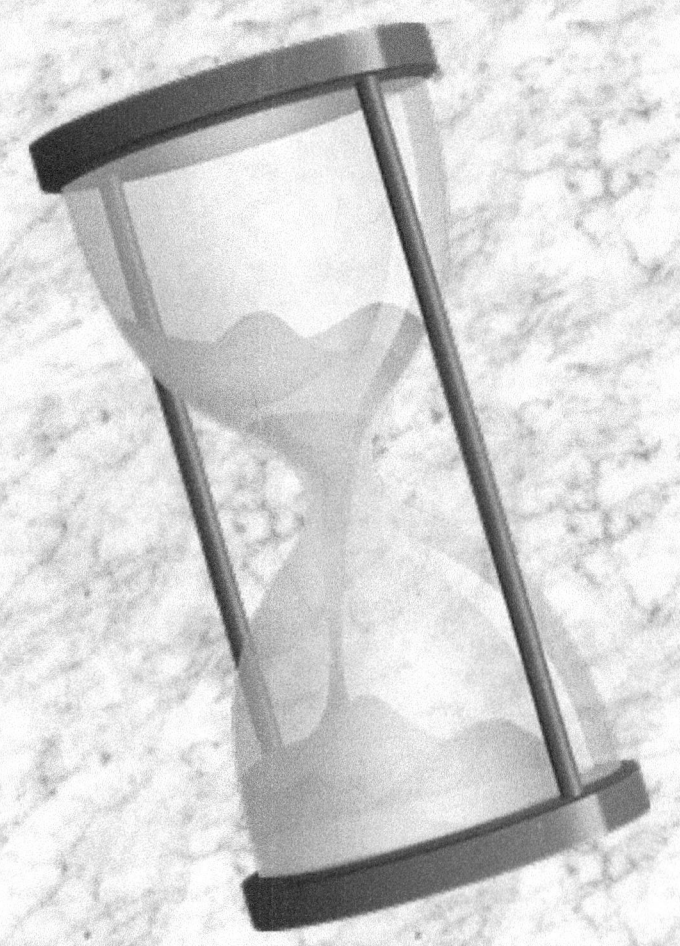

Am I holding on to something I need to let go of?

What am I doing about the things that matter most in my life?

Have I made someone smile today?

What have I given up on?

When did I last step out of my comfort zone?

What is life calling on me to do?

What small act of kindness was I once shown that I will never forget?

Am I achieving the goals that I've set for myself?

Am I trying?

How can I love myself more today?

What advice would you give to yourself 10 years ago?

What's stopping you?

What are you doing about it?

Are they helping you to get where you want to go?

How can I be more engaged in my life?

How can I live more authentically?

Are my choices based on "I should" rather than "I desire"?

Am I behaving as a reactor rather than an initiator?

How am I letting fear direct my life?

In what ways do I put down other people to make myself feel better?

Where am I holding back forgiveness?

What negative thoughts am I still holding on to?

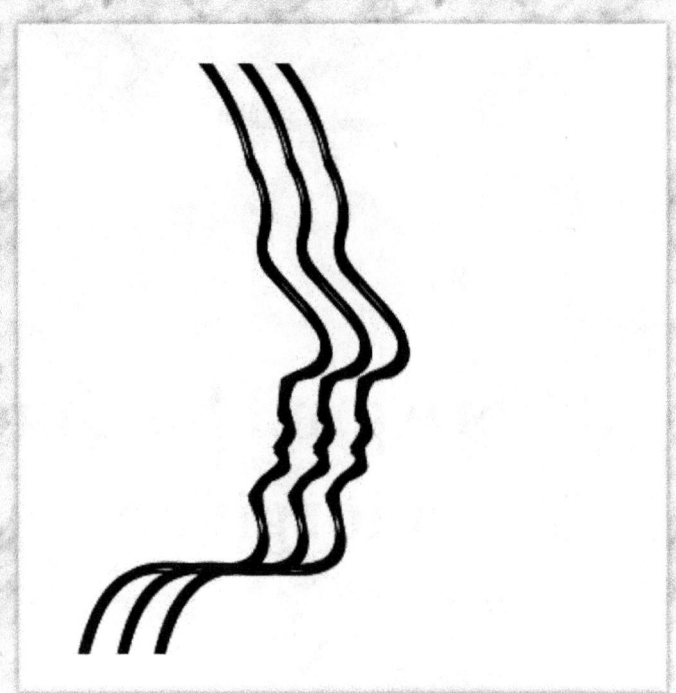

How do I allow other people to cross my boundaries?

When possible
Be fully present

Don't get caught up in other people's problems?

Am I making it more complicated than it has to be?

Is it entertainment or distraction?

Am I mistreating my body or compromising my health?

What do I feel passionate about?

Do I spend too much time worrying about the future?

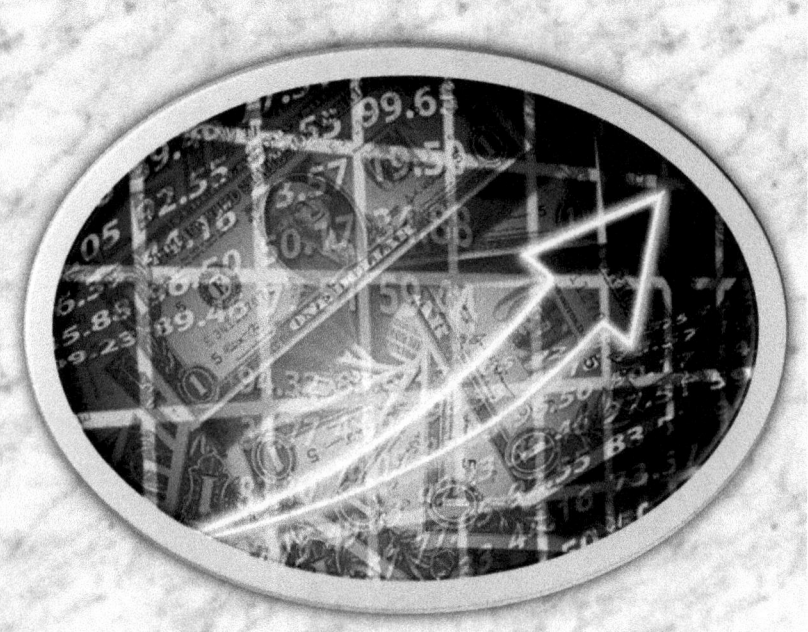

What events from my past are hindering my ability to live in the present?

Why do I feel like I'm not worthy?

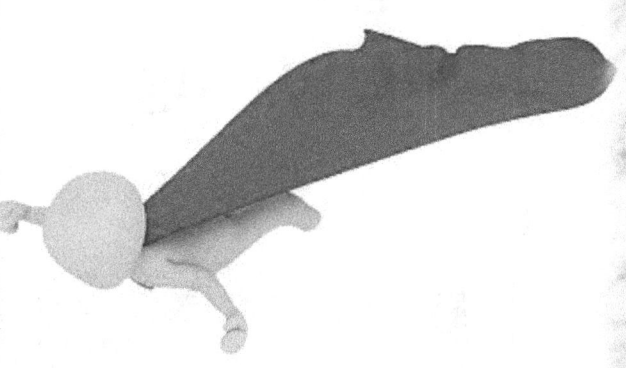

Am I waiting for someone else to solve my problems?

What is my intuition telling me that I'm ignoring?

What really pushes my buttons that doesn't need to?

onlyloveonlyloveonlylove onlyloveonlyloveonlylove

Only Love

Only Love

Only Love

Only Love

Only Love

Only Love

How am I being irresponsible with money?

Am I hesitant to show or express love?

What expectations do I have for my kids that are more for me than them?

What's the next step in my personal growth?

Am I enjoying the journey?

Why
So
Angry

Your father was wrong

Bend as needed
NEVER, EVER break

If you look for beauty you will surely find it

Your mother was wrong

Read the signs

You're looking for the key to the universe

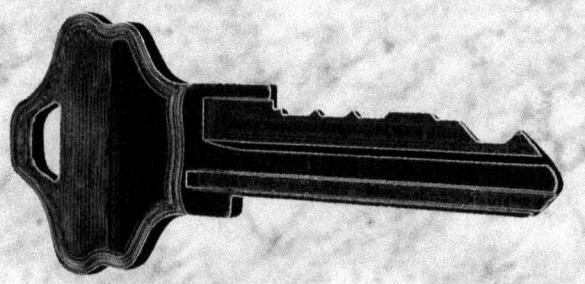

BUT IT AIN'T LOCKED

Thanks George

For additional copies please contact
Gary Pignatello at
gary@indistrictsolutions.com

Copy only with written permission from the author

©2017 Gary Pignatello All Rights Reserved

www.ingramcontent.com/pod-product-compliance
Lightning Source LLC
Chambersburg PA
CBHW060159050426
42446CB00013B/2911